Parlor Guitar

by Joel Mabus

ISBN-13: 978-1-4234-1251-9
ISBN-10: 1-4234-1251-6

HAL•LEONARD®
CORPORATION
7777 W. BLUEMOUND RD. P.O. BOX 13819 MILWAUKEE, WI 53213

In Australia Contact:
Hal Leonard Australia Pty. Ltd.
4 Lentara Court
Cheltenham, Victoria, 3192 Australia
Email: ausadmin@halleonard.com

Visit Hal Leonard Online at
www.halleonard.com

Preface

People have always enjoyed music in their homes. Every culture has had its folksongs and homemade tunes passed down from earlier generations. But a century ago, even before radio broadcasting made it commonplace, composed popular music also had a place in the American home—usually played from sheet music. Much of this "parlor music" drew from the musical theater, vaudeville, and other stagecraft. Such is the case with this collection.

It's easy to admire these well-crafted melodies. They speak to the genius of another age, and they really do stand up strong after all these years. But as it happens, none of them were written with the guitar in mind. That allows the guitar arranger to work from a clean slate. In each of these pieces, I have tried to balance my respect for the composer's work with a desire to let the guitar sing in its own language, striving for something fresh, yet informed.

Considering its current popularity, it is hard to imagine a time when the guitar was rarely played in concert, but originally the guitar was meant for an intimate audience rather than the public stage. A hundred years ago, the petite shape of what is now called the "parlor guitar" was considered the full and proper size for the instrument. Lighter in touch and more balanced in tone than most of the larger models of today, the sweet voice of the steel-stringed parlor guitar is particularly suited for fingerstyle playing.

The transcriptions in this book are taken note-for-note from my album of the same name. The accompanying CD has selections from the original disc. The guitar I play on these recordings (a maple-bodied Larrivée parlor model) was built quite recently, but very much in the tradition of guitars a century earlier. In happy synchronicity, the hi-tech studio where these songs were performed (Arcadia Recording) is housed in the front parlor of a grand Victorian home in Kalamazoo, Michigan, a city long known for its guitars. Recorded in the first four days of summer, 2005, the parlor guitar felt right at home in the acoustics of the parlor studio, celebrating some wonderful old parlor music.

The ten songs in this folio are a nice sample from the melting pot of immigrant America. The biographies of Jerome Kern, George Gershwin, and Irving Berlin are well-known, and early breakthrough hits of these three giants of popular music are given here—"They Didn't Believe Me," "Swanee," and "Alexander's Ragtime Band." Notice that the last two were both written with musical nods to an earlier songwriting icon—Stephen Foster and his "Old Folks at Home."

"Tishomingo Blues" is from Spencer Williams, a prolific African-American composer and pianist originally from New Orleans. He wrote this number about a sleepy Mississippi town while living in New York in 1918, a few years before he immigrated to Europe to escape racial discrimination.

"Sobre las olas" is a Mexican waltz, know in English as "Over the Waves." It made a big splash (no pun intended) at the New Orleans World's Fair in 1884 when played by its 16-year-old composer, violinist Juventino Rosas. Rosas was of the native Otomi people, making this melody not only the oldest of the collection, but the only one from an indigenous American.

A German composer, Paul Lincke, wrote "The Glow Worm" for his 1902 operetta, *Lysistrata*. A worldwide sensation, it was interpolated into the 1907 New York show, *Girl Behind the Counter*, with an English translation. About 40 years later, the lyric got a rewrite by Johnny Mercer for the show's movie version. It was Mercer's new lyric that fed the Mills Brothers' hit record in the 1940s. "Paper Doll" was another hit for the Mills, a number written by vaudeville showman and pianist Johnny S. Black in 1915. I recorded these two songs in medley; the intro to "The Glow Worm" works as the modulation between them.

Al Jolson introduced "April Showers" in his smash 1921 show, *Bombo*, in the guise of his familiar blackface alter ego, Gus. The song's composer, Louis Silvers, conducted the orchestra in the pit. Of the many songs made hits by Jolson, this one later became his designated theme song on radio. Silvers went on to a successful career scoring movies in Hollywood.

"Tiger Rag" is credited to Nick La Rocca, the head of the Original Dixieland Jass Band that recorded it in 1917. But the tune, with its several themes, is really a folk song by most definitions. All the strains were well-known to New Orleans street musicians as anonymous creations and some can be traced to old French quadrilles. La Rocca and the ODJB were first to record this boisterous early jazz anthem, sometimes called "Hold That Tiger."

The title may surprise you, but "Grand Old Rag" is indeed the original name of George M. Cohan's rousing "Grand Old Flag." Early critics forced him to change the title and lyric after its debut in his 1906 musical, *George Washington Jr.* In the play, an old Confederate veteran looked on the Yankee flag and admitted, "She's a grand old rag after all!" This flag-waving number ensued—a clever play on words, considering the ragtime era was in full swing. As either "rag" or "flag," it is a lot of fun to play on the guitar.

With all these transcriptions, I have used standard notation in the top staff and tablature below. Written as two voices—thumb and fingers—all the down-pointing stems are played by the thumb as down-strokes. The up-pointing stems are played by the fingers as up-strokes unless otherwise indicated. Hammer-ons, pull-offs, and slides are notated with slurs or glissando markings on the top staff and also in the tablature. The chord names above the top staff are there to help you understand the harmonization and can act as an aid to improvising or for accompaniment. In some cases, the notation will not have you fingering a typical voicing of the chord. If you are working from the top staff and question the fingering, a glance to the tab staff should help.

You certainly don't need a small-bodied parlor guitar to play these arrangements, but a slightly shorter fretboard might be helpful on a few of the longer stretches. For small hands on a large guitar, you might try a capo at the second fret. It would approximate the scale length of a parlor guitar and make the reach a bit easier.

I hope you enjoy playing these songs in your own parlor as much as I do. Happy fingering!

Joel Mabus

Dedication & Gratitude

Thanks to John Stites, who made the recording process seem so easy, and to
Stan and the gang at Elderly Instruments for support over the years.

This book is dedicated to my wife Jan, who has lived with this project from start
to finish—and listened to these tunes a thousand times—with no complaints.

They Didn't Believe Me

Jerome Kern 1914

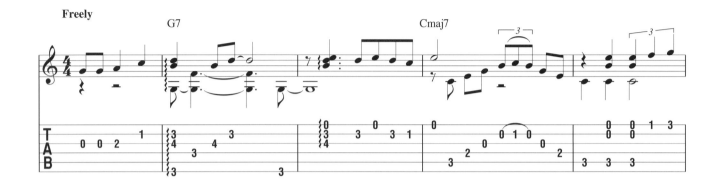

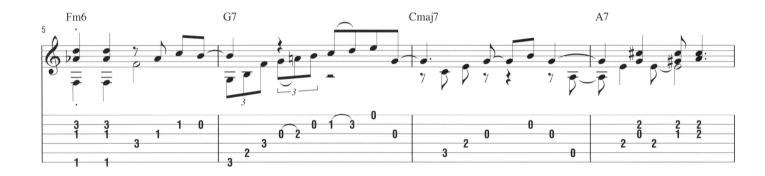

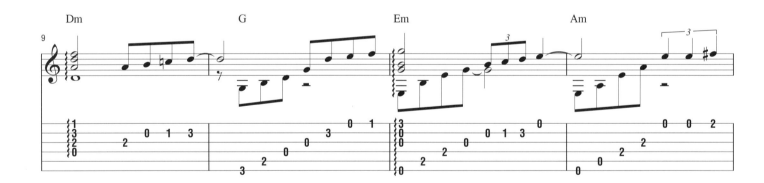

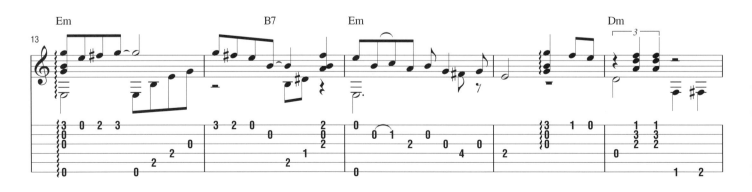

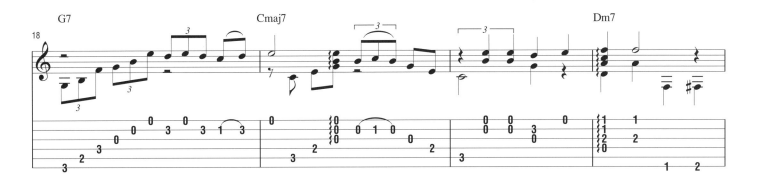

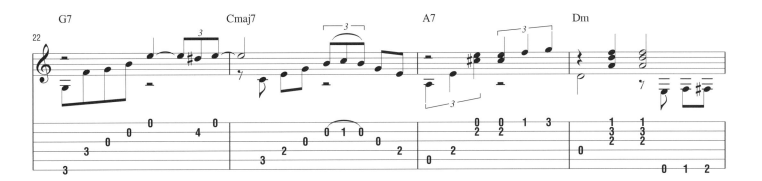

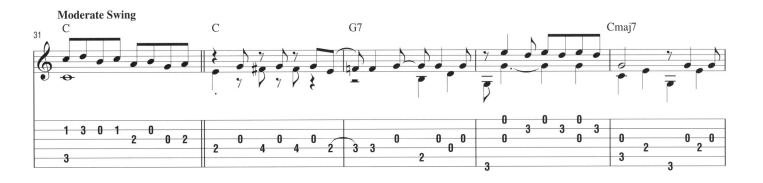

Moderate Swing

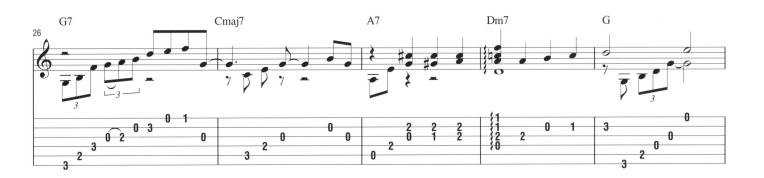

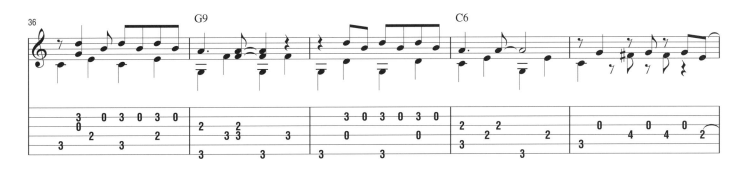

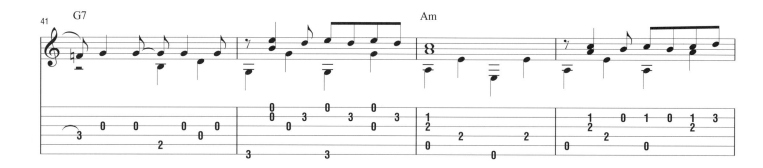

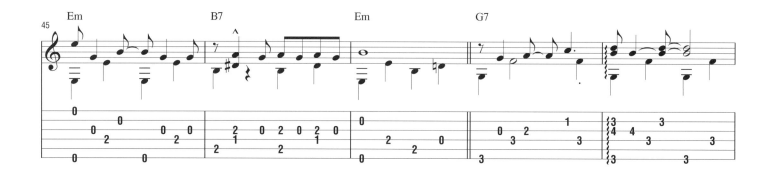

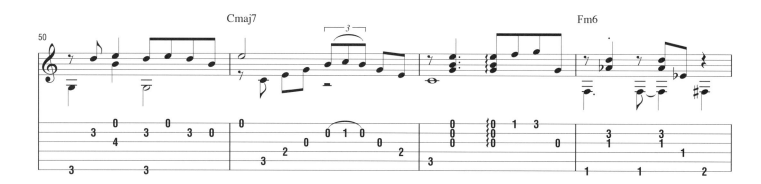

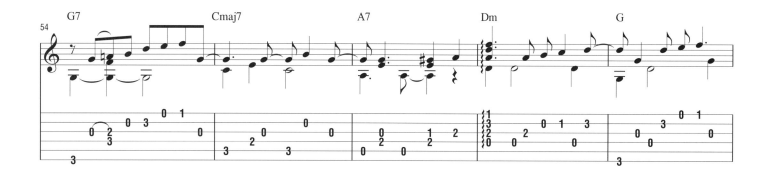

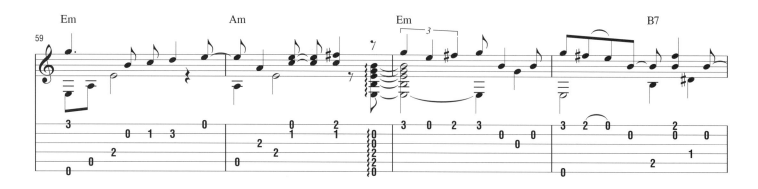

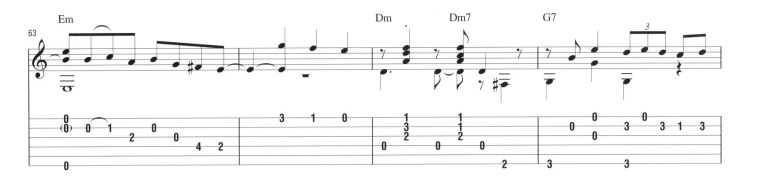

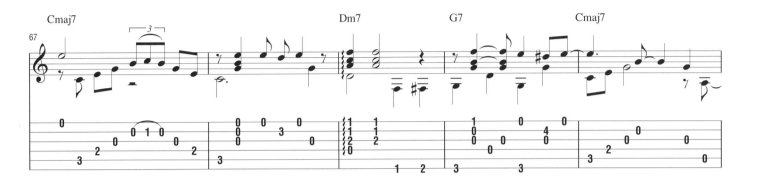

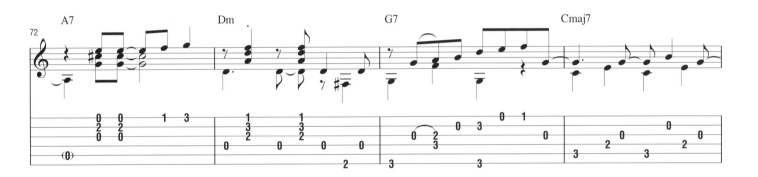

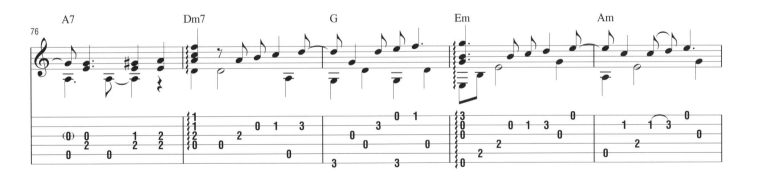

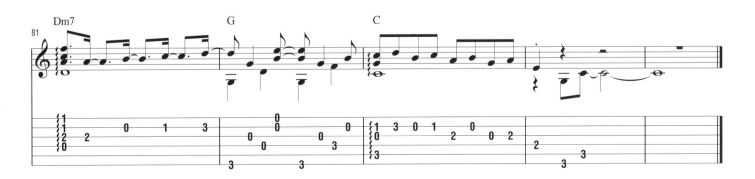

Swanee

George Gershwin 1919

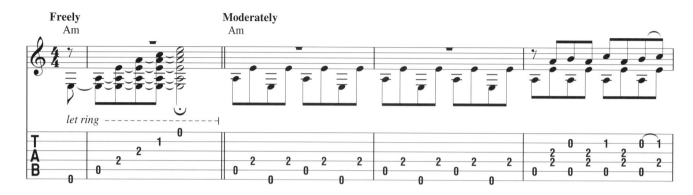

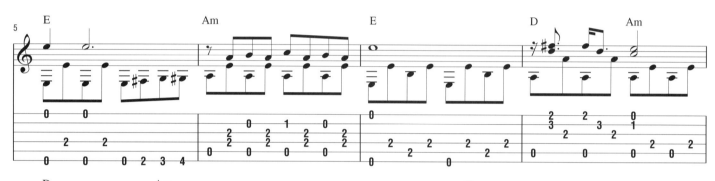

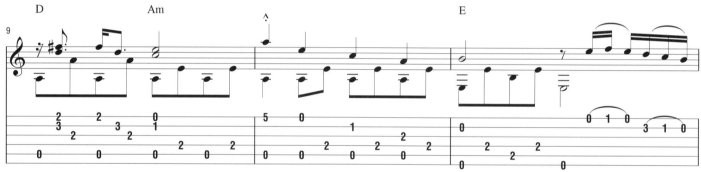

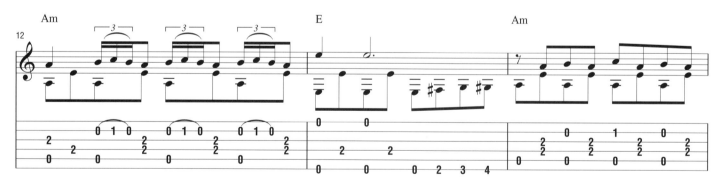

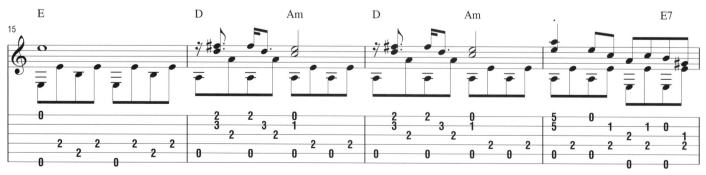

8

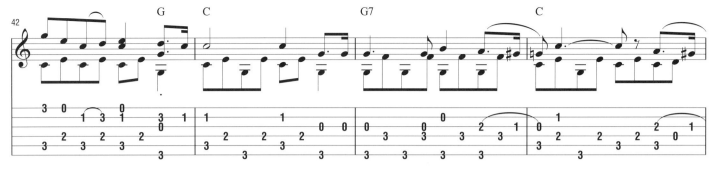

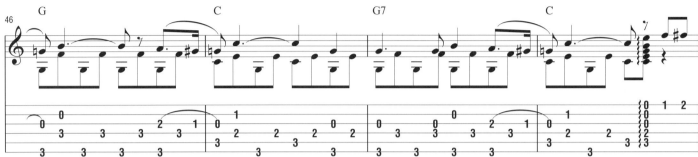

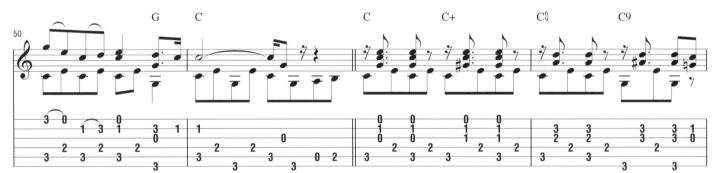

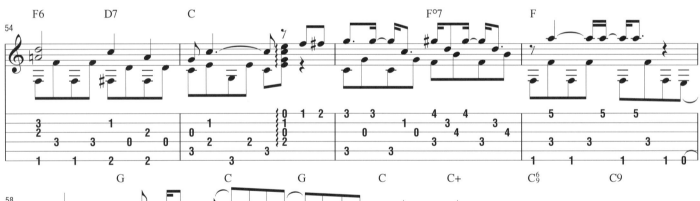

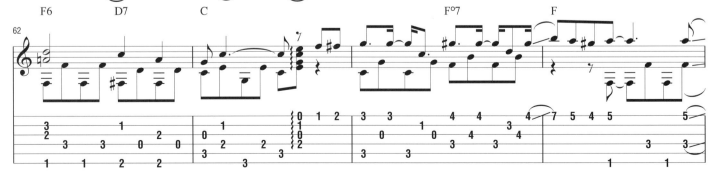

Tishomingo Blues

Spencer Williams 1918

TRACK 3

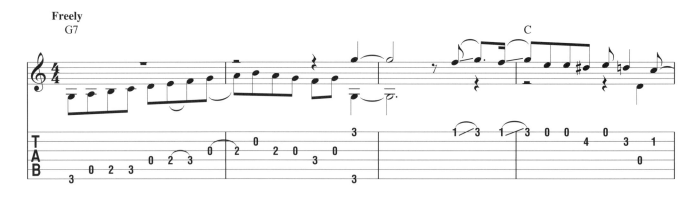

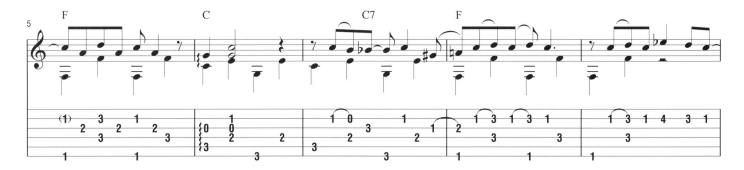

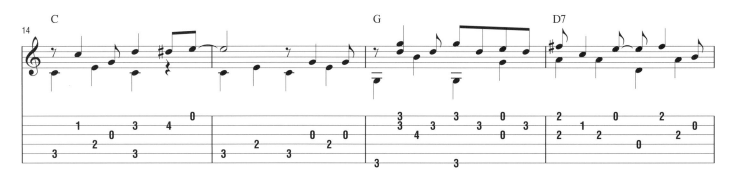

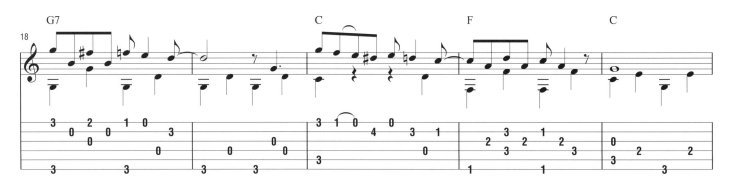

Arrangement © 2006 by Joel Mabus
All Rights Reserved

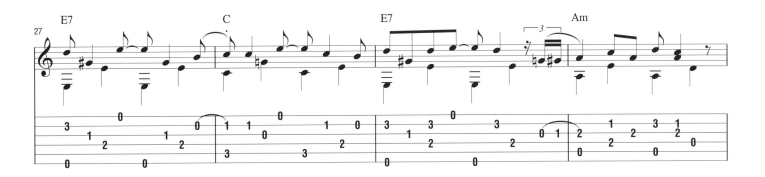

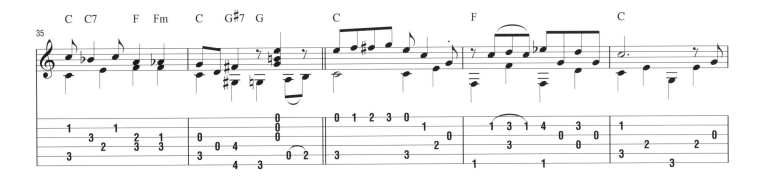

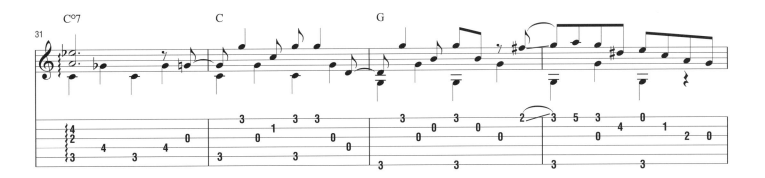

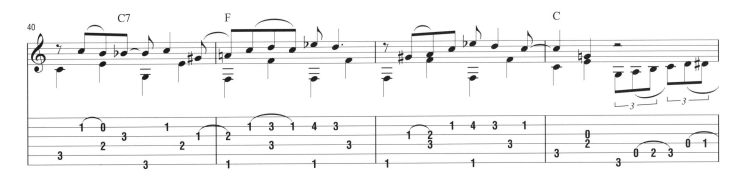

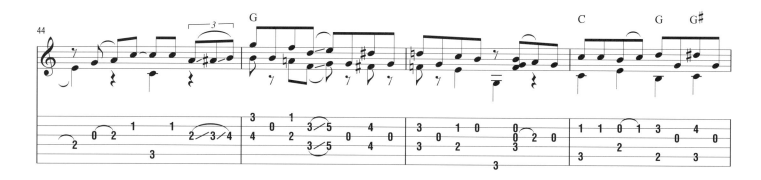

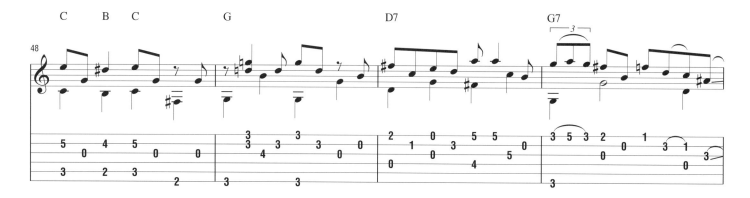

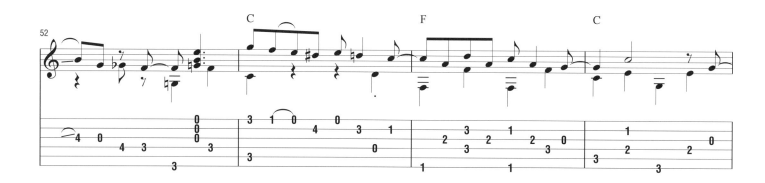

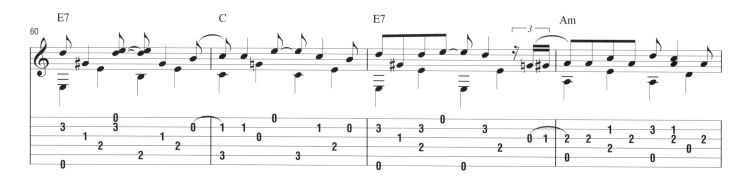

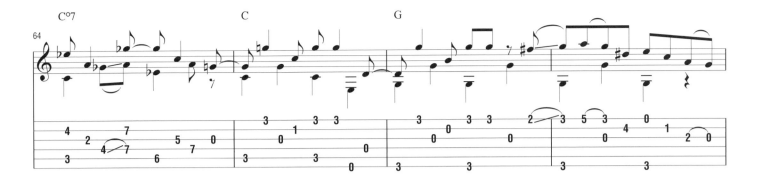

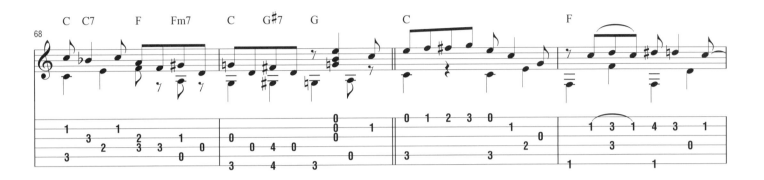

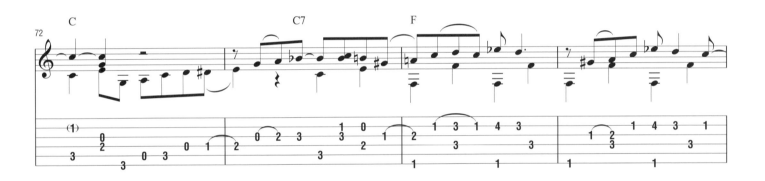

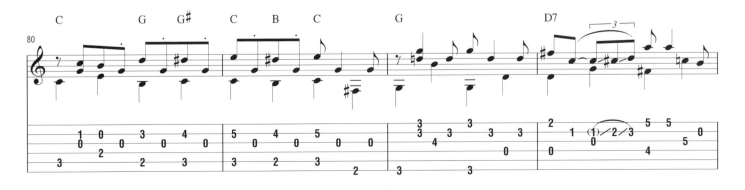

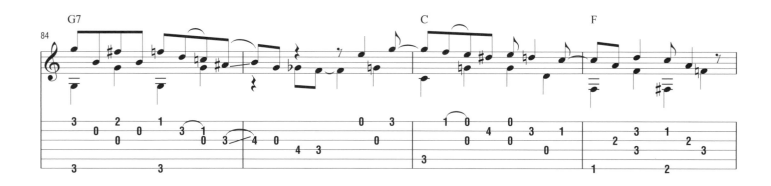

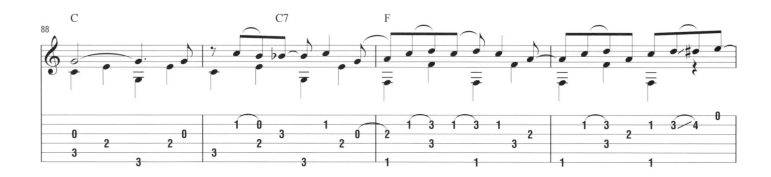

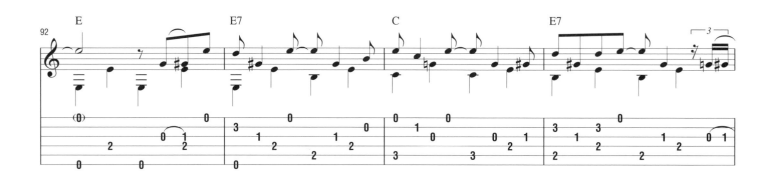

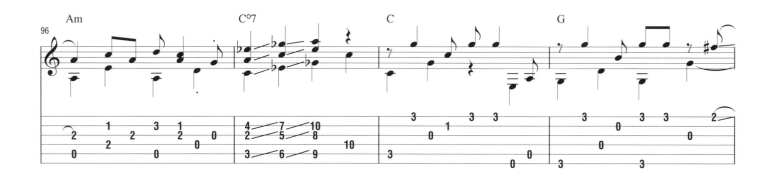

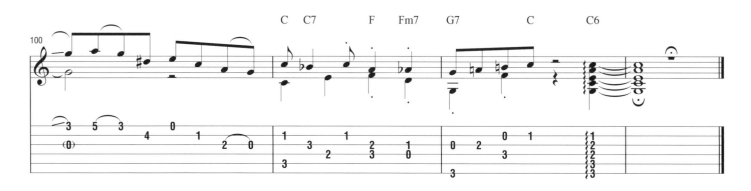

Sobre las olas
(Over the Waves)

Juventino Rosas 1884

Moderate Waltz

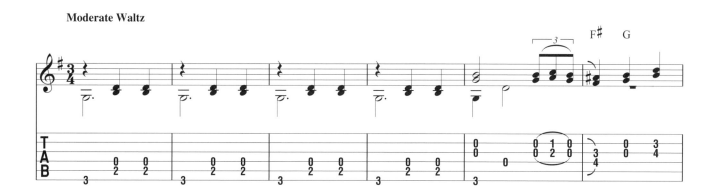

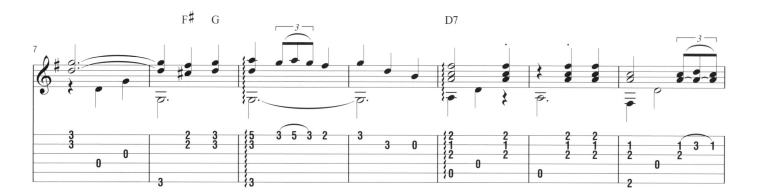

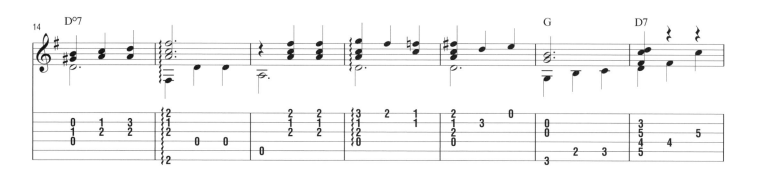

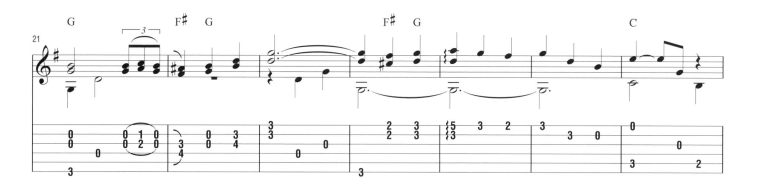

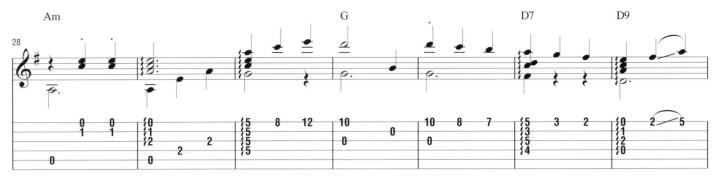

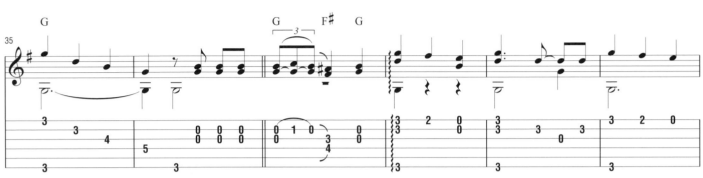

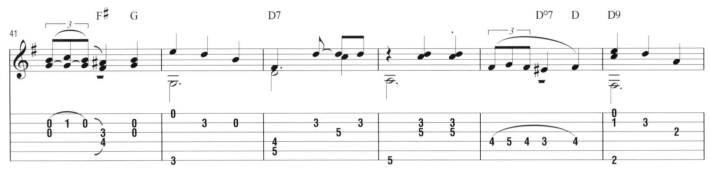

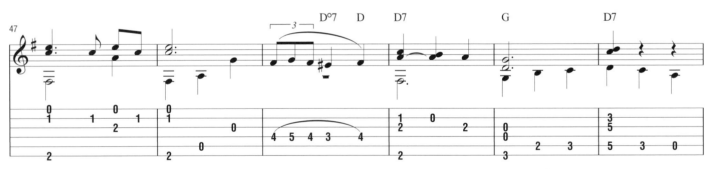

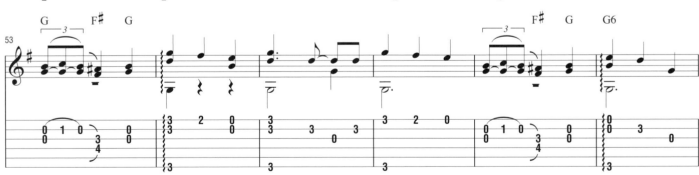

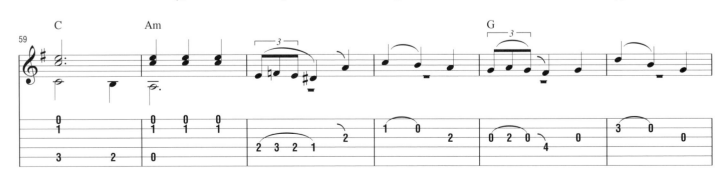

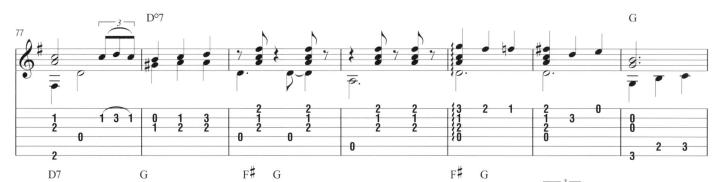

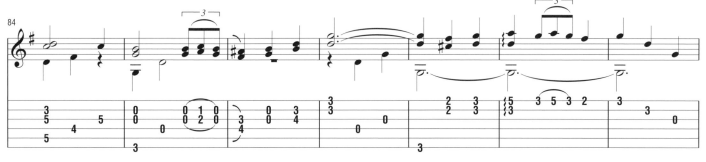

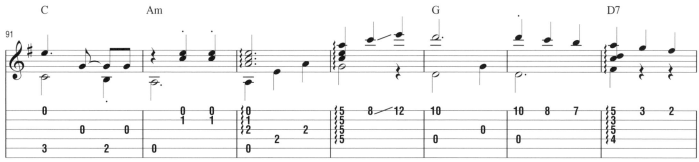

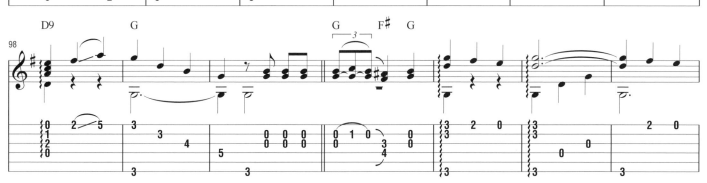

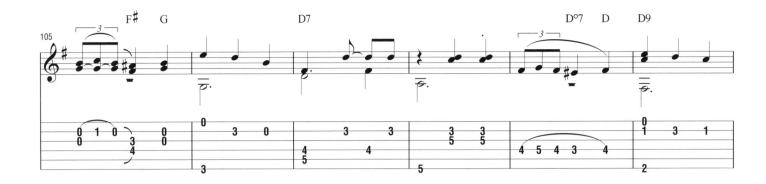

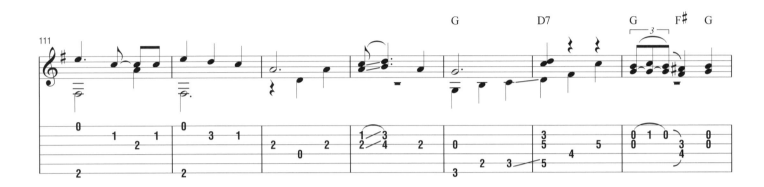

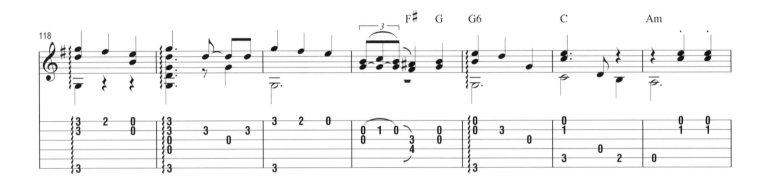

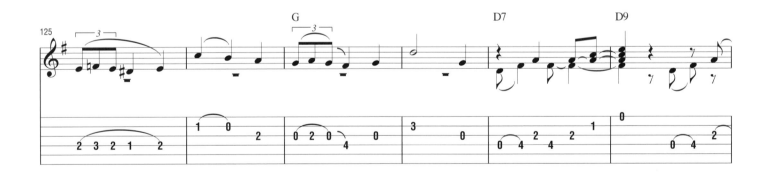

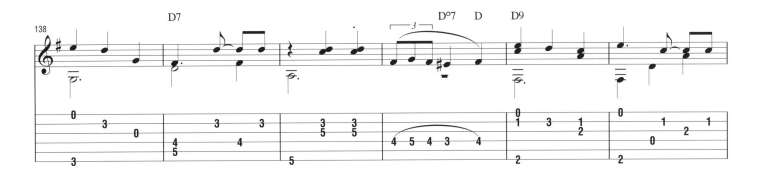

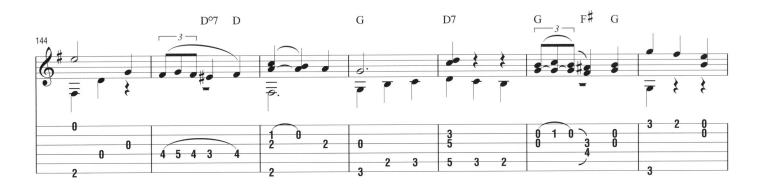

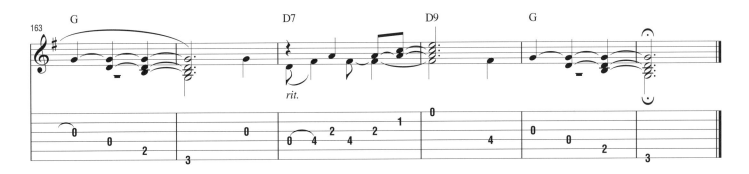

Paper Doll

Johnny S. Black 1915

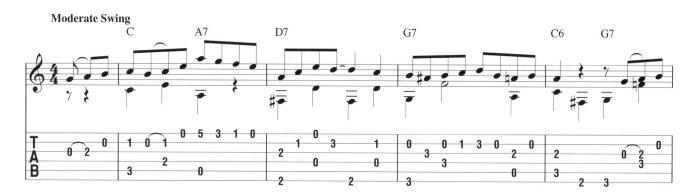

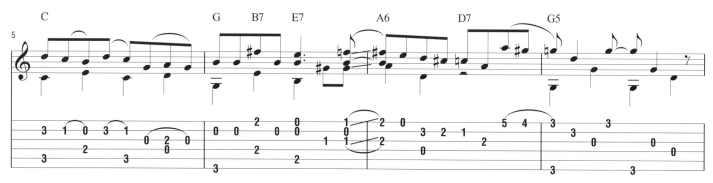

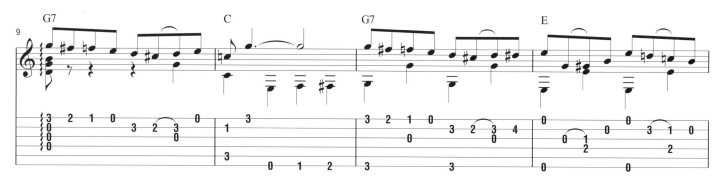

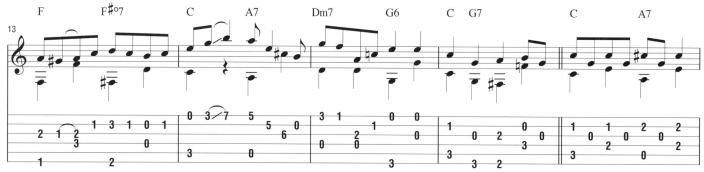

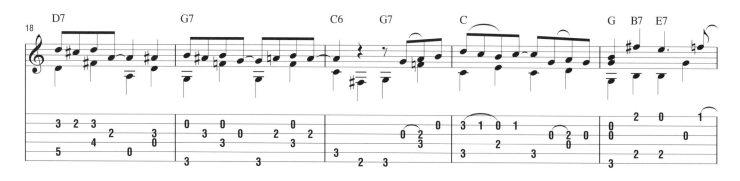

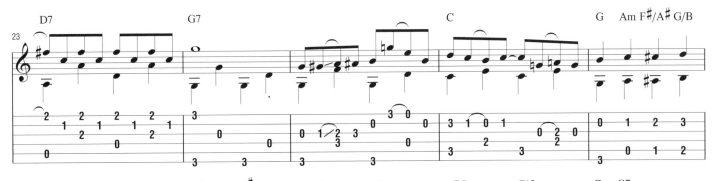

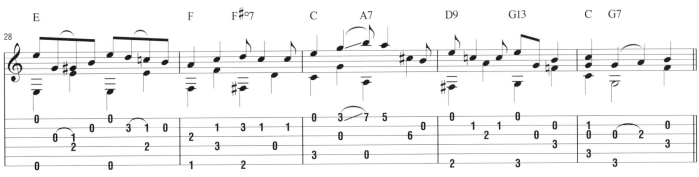

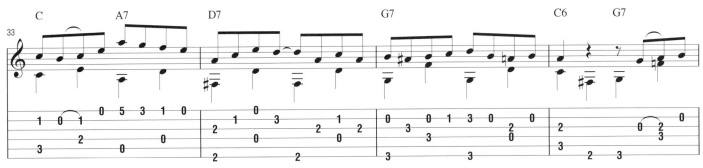

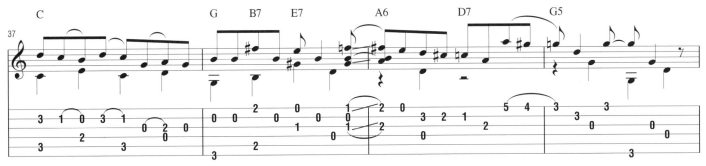

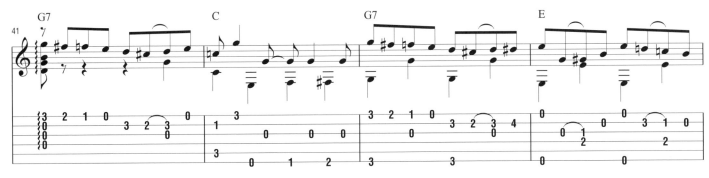

Segue to
"The Glow Worm"

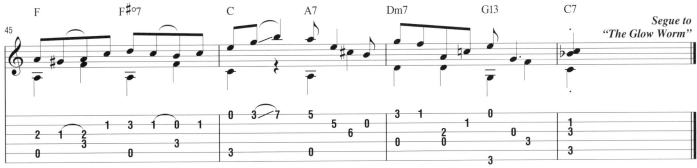

The Glow Worm

Paul Lincke 1902

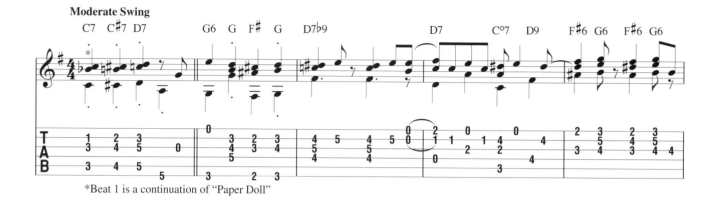

*Beat 1 is a continuation of "Paper Doll"

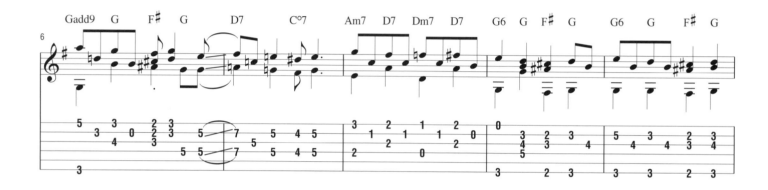

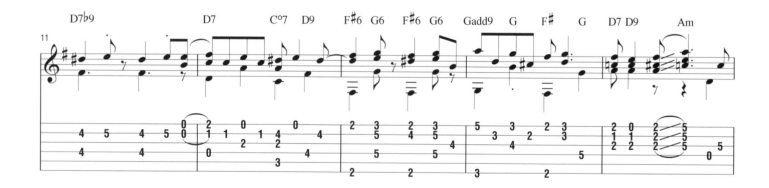

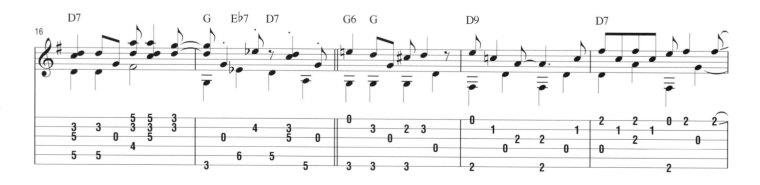

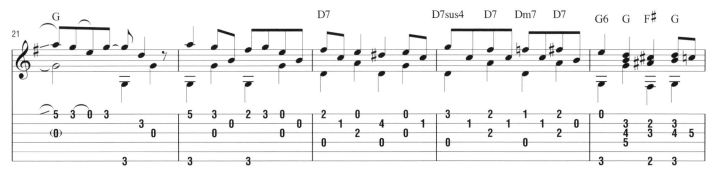

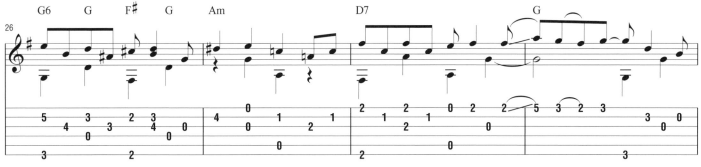

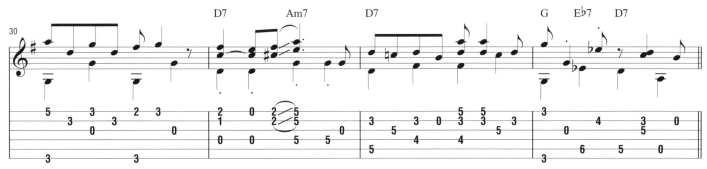

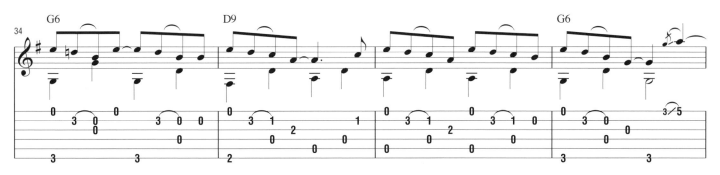

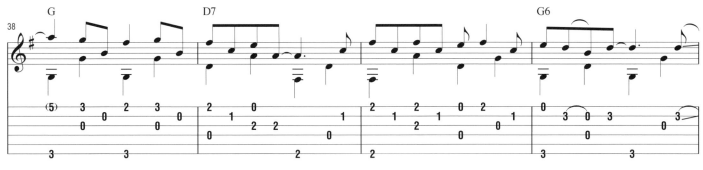

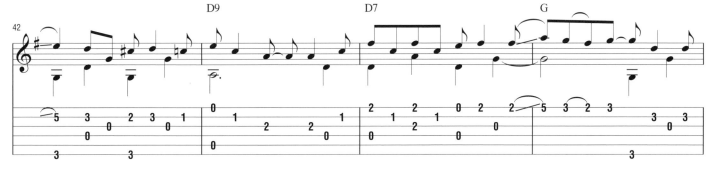

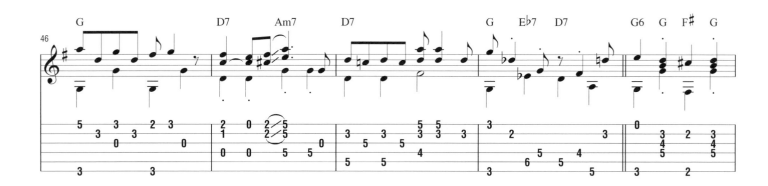

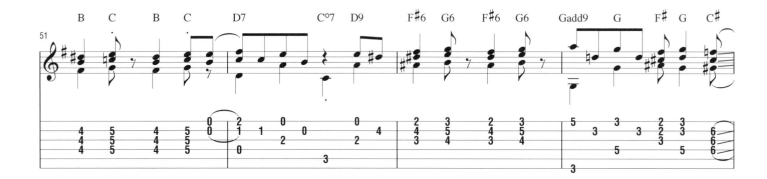

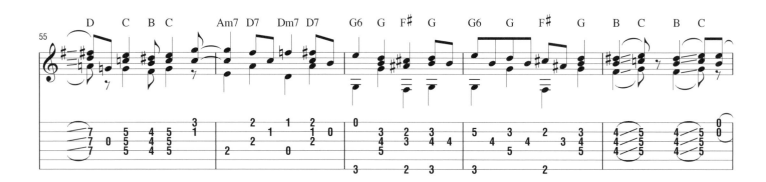

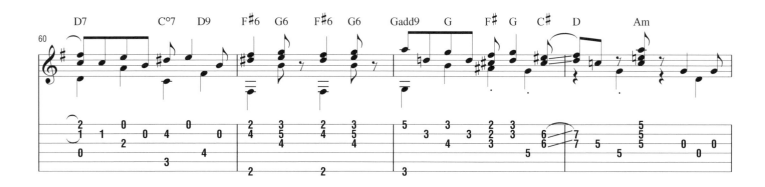

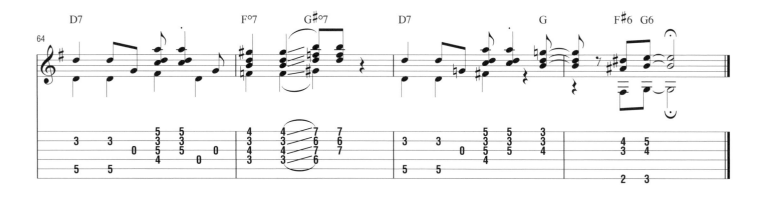

Alexander's Ragtime Band

Irving Berlin 1911

TRACK 6

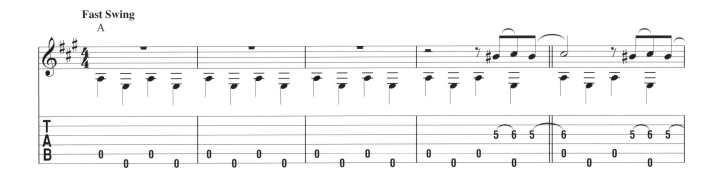

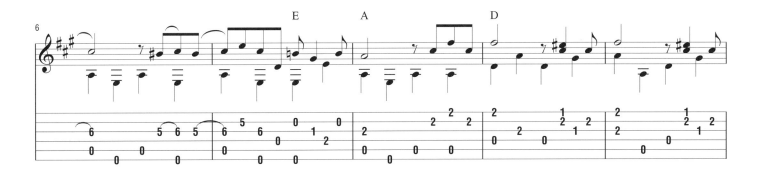

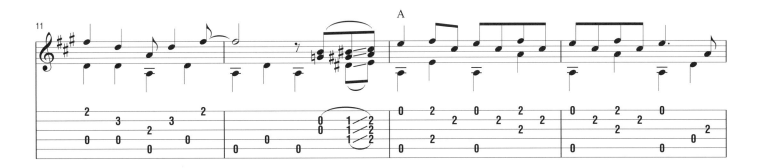

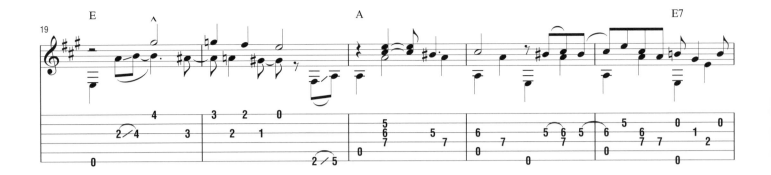

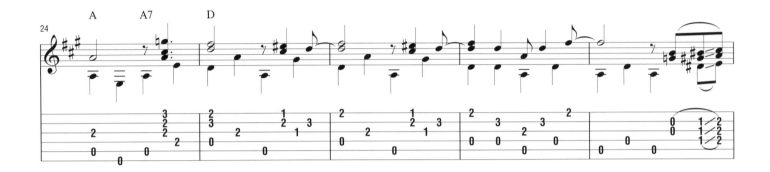

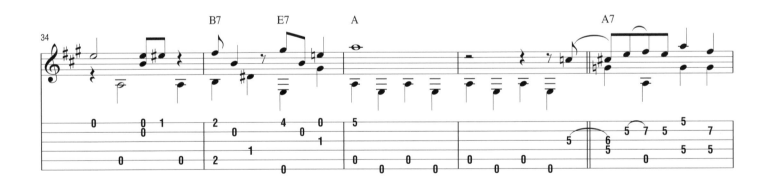

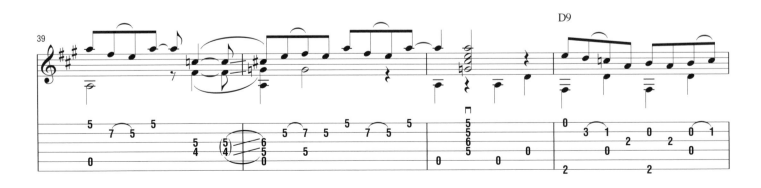

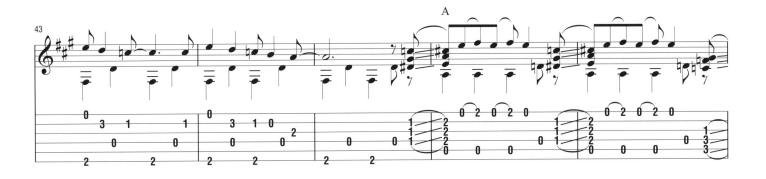

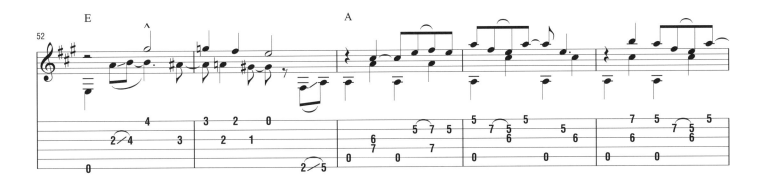

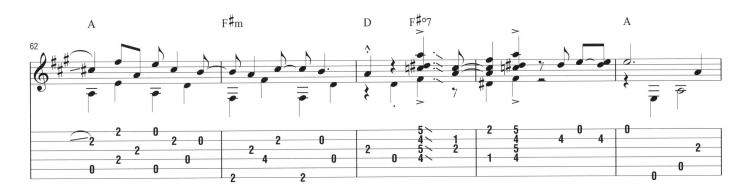

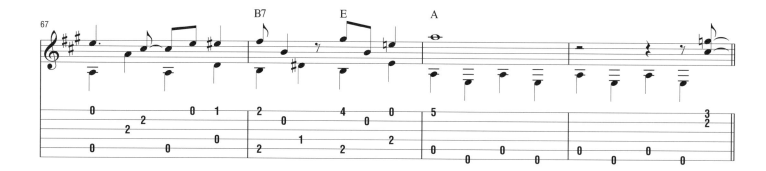

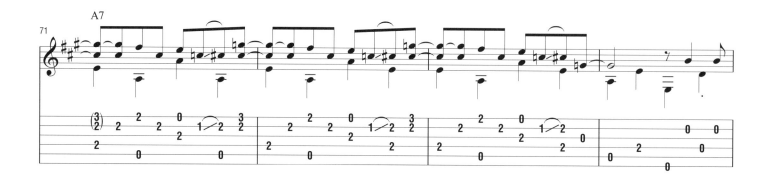

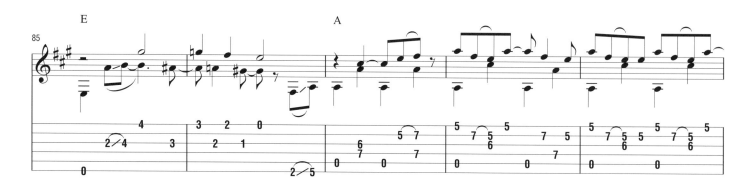

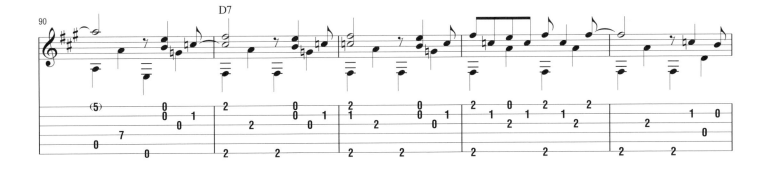

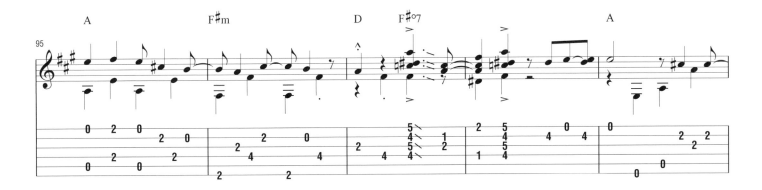

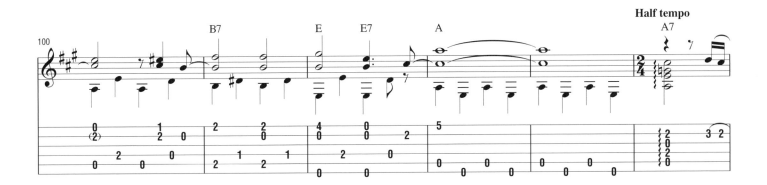

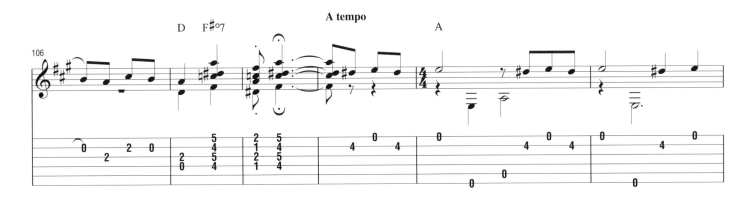

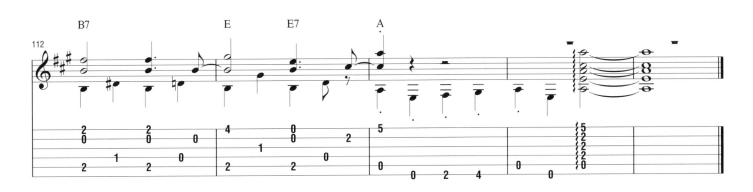

Tiger Rag
(Hold That Tiger)

Nick La Rocca, et al 1917

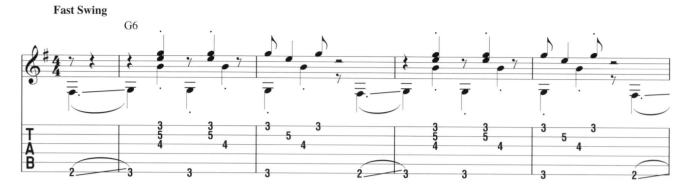

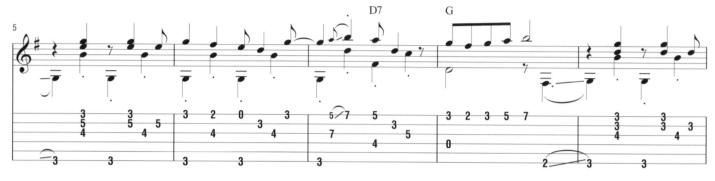

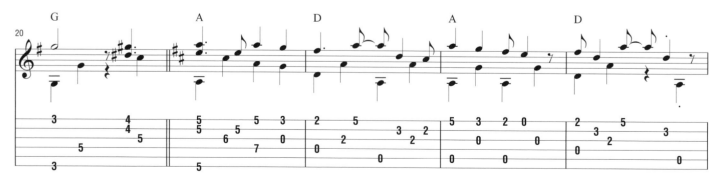

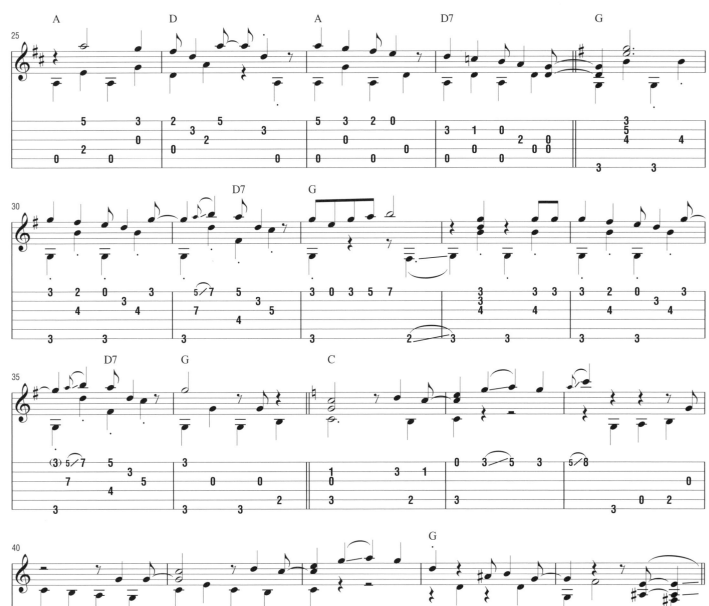
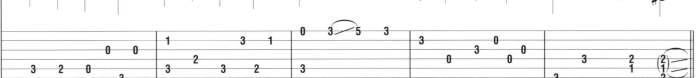
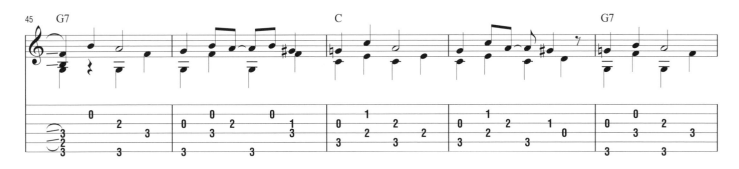
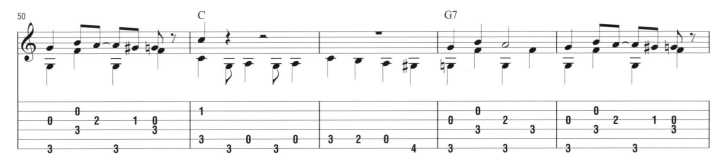

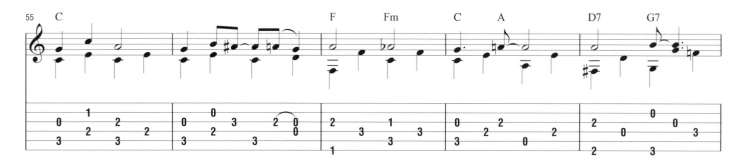

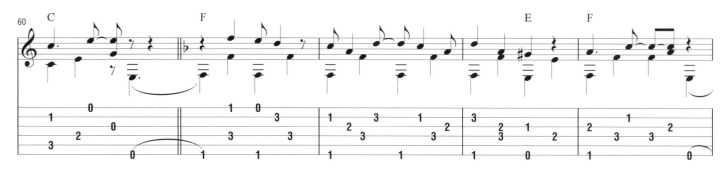

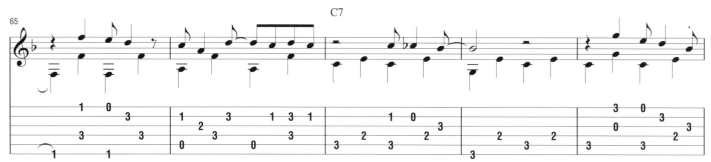

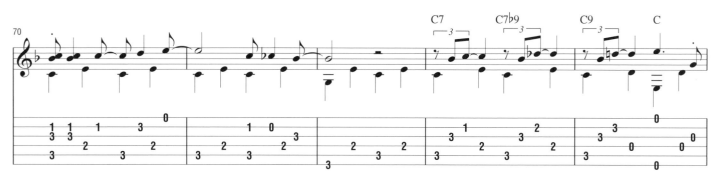

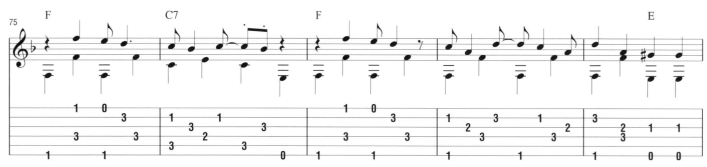

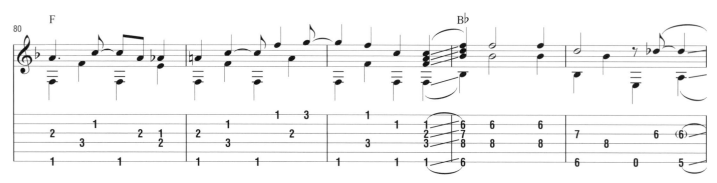

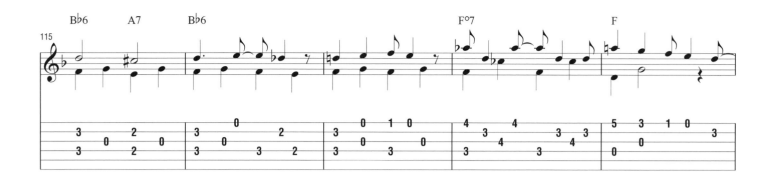

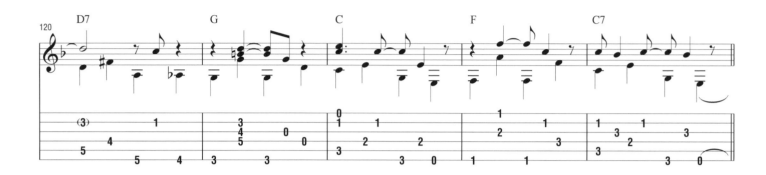

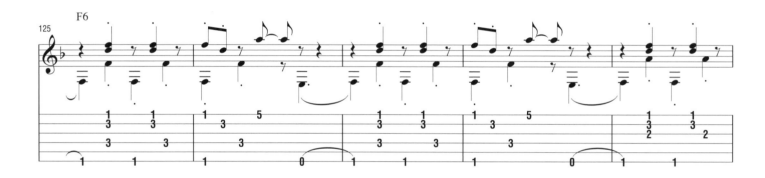

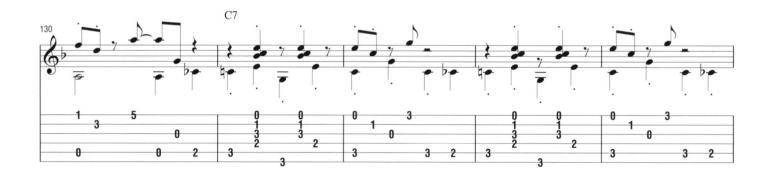

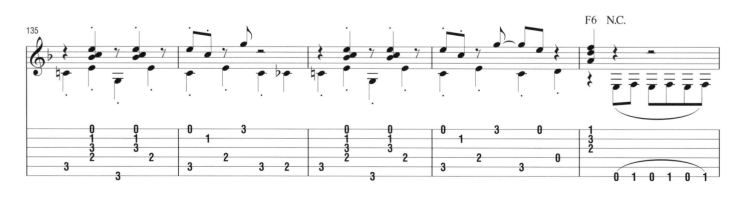

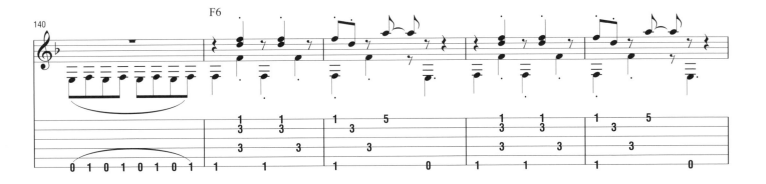

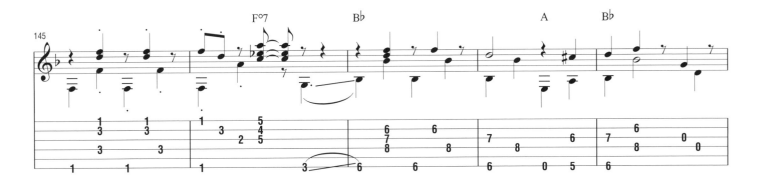

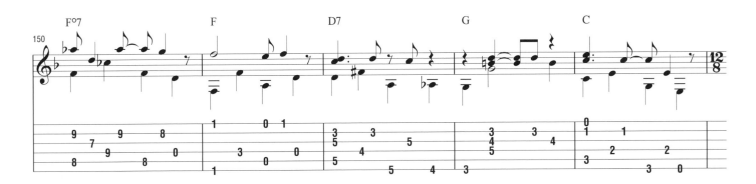

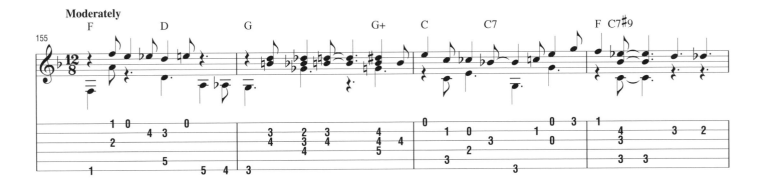

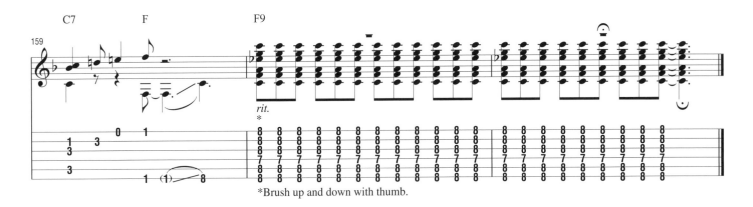

*Brush up and down with thumb.

Grand Old Rag

George M. Cohan 1906

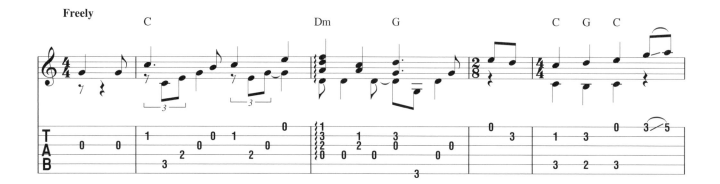

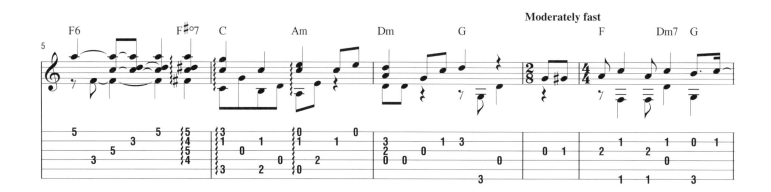

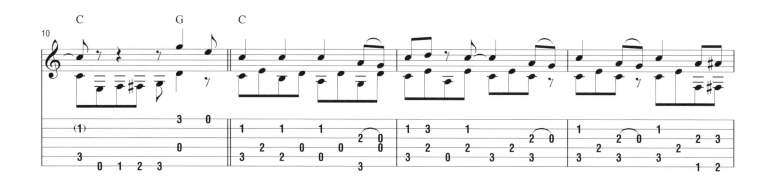

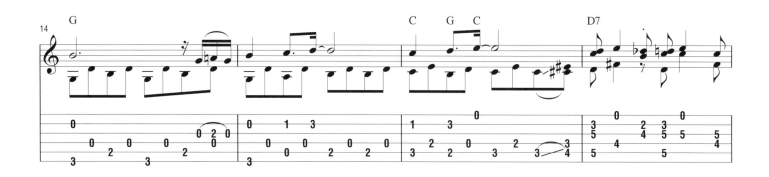

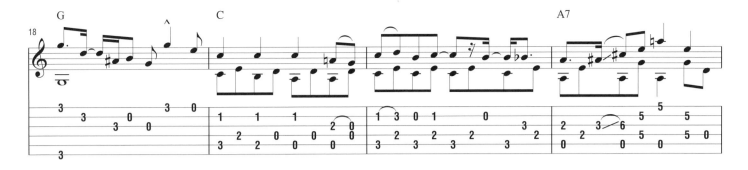

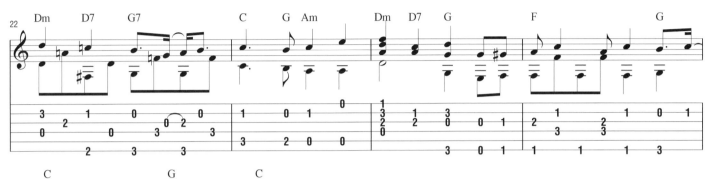

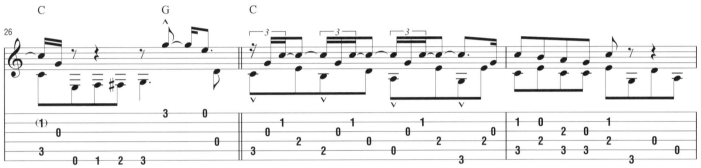

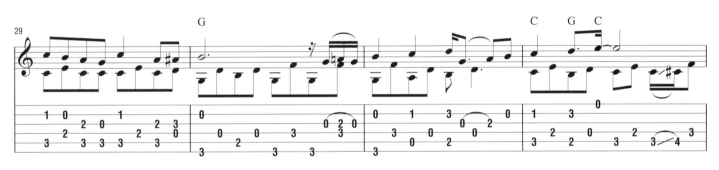

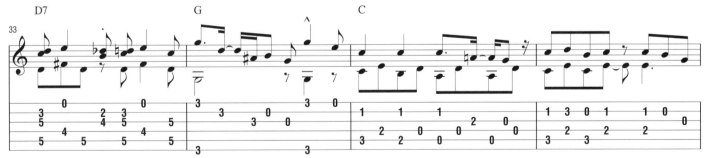

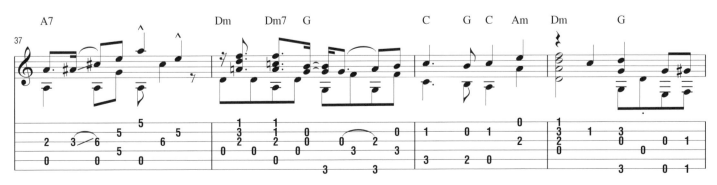

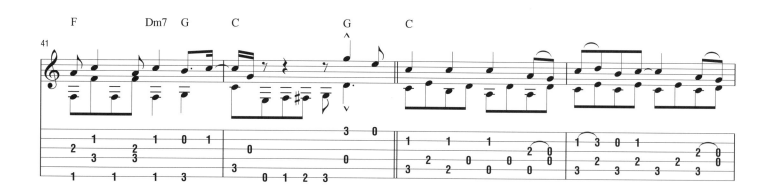

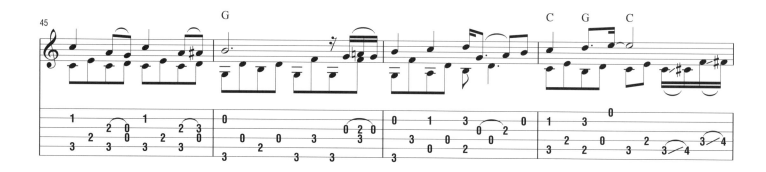

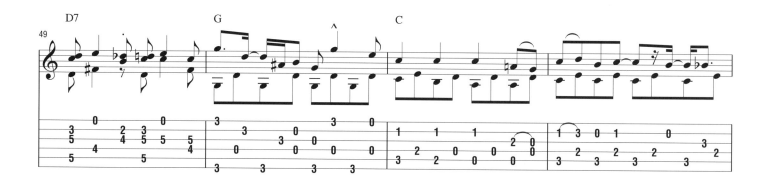

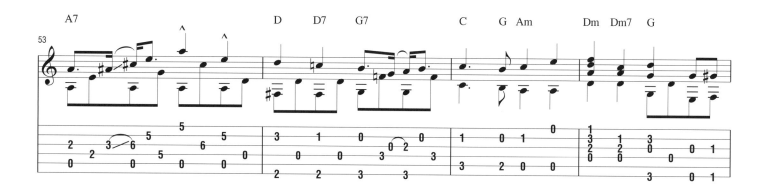

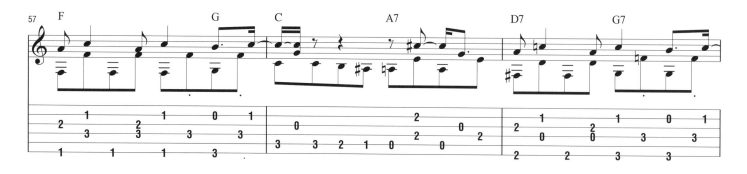

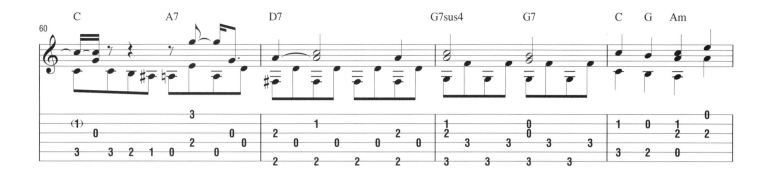

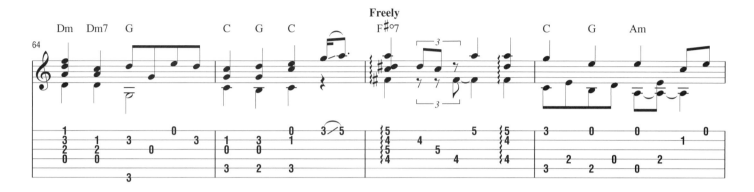

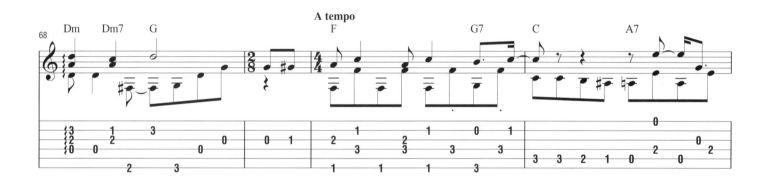

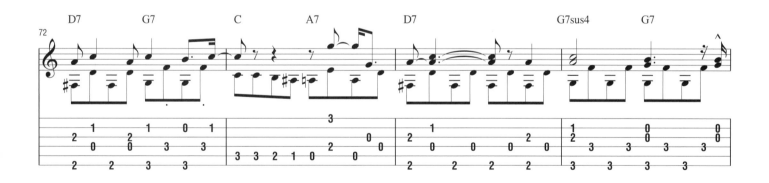

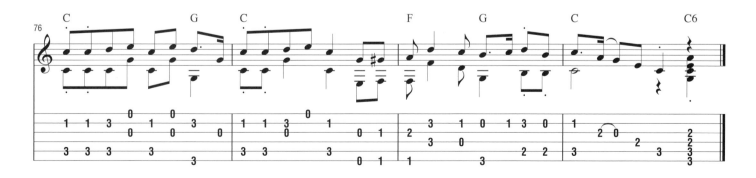

April Showers

Louis Silvers 1921

TRACK 7

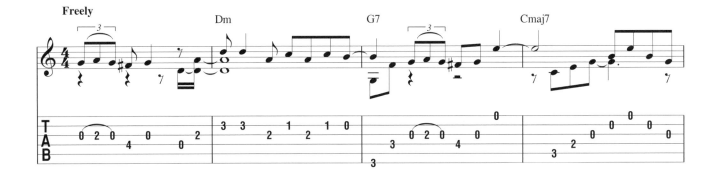

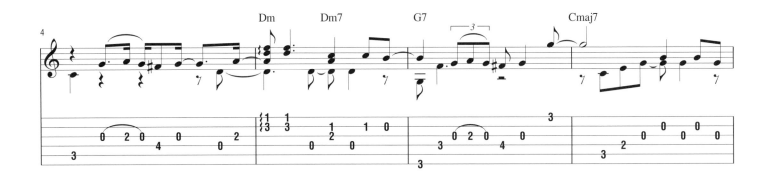

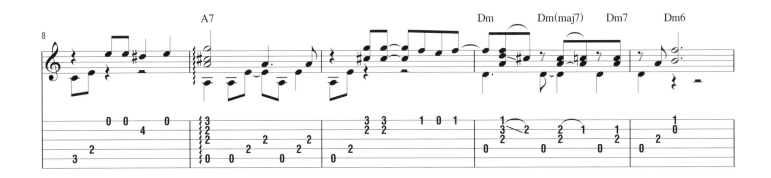

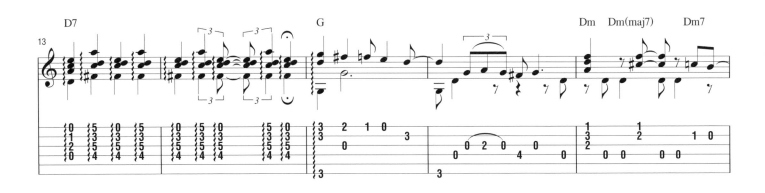

Arrangement © 2006 by Joel Mabus
All Rights Reserved

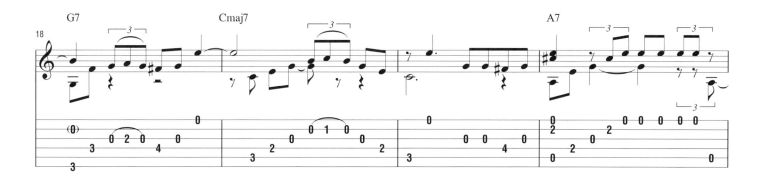

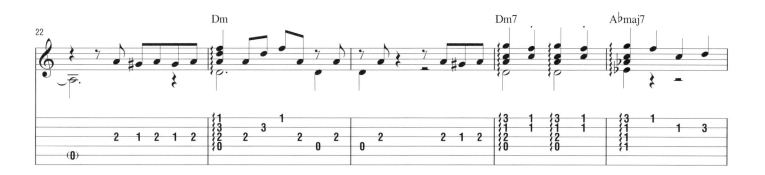

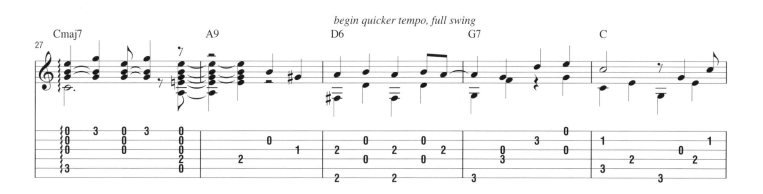

begin quicker tempo, full swing

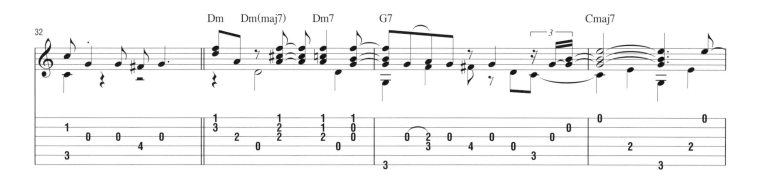

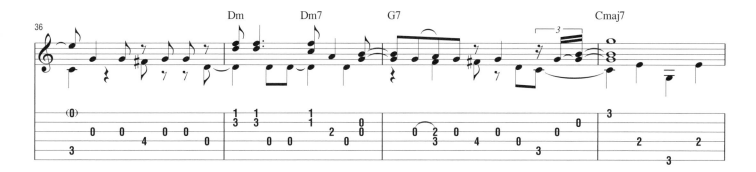

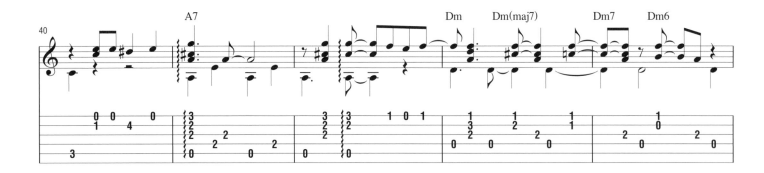

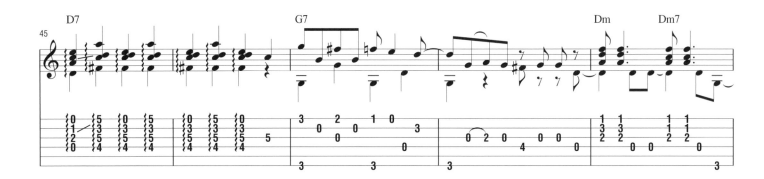

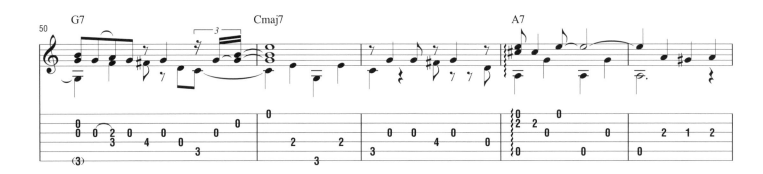

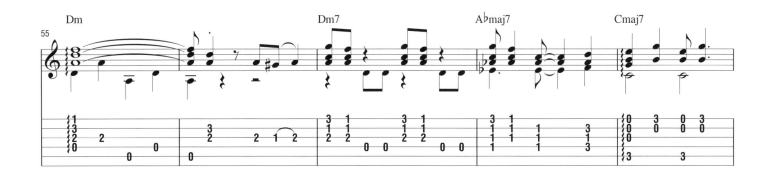

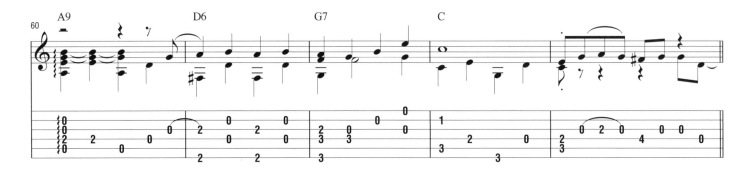

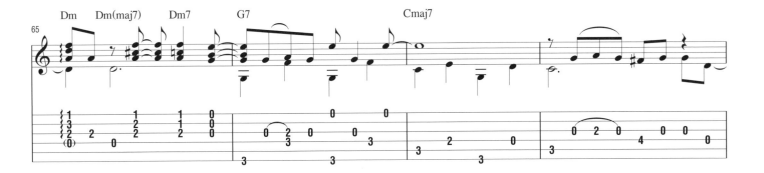

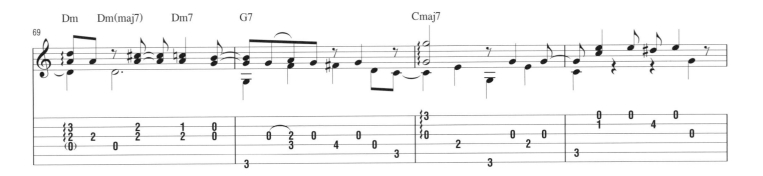

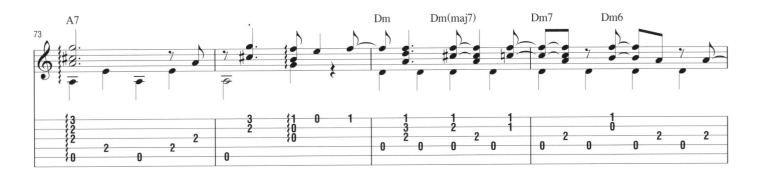

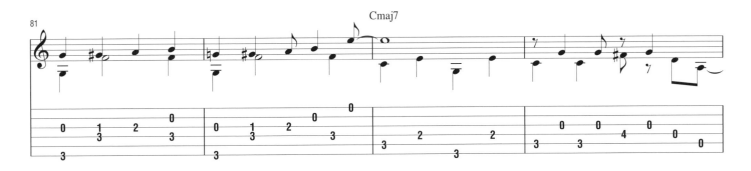

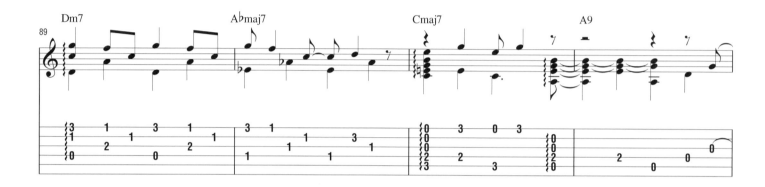

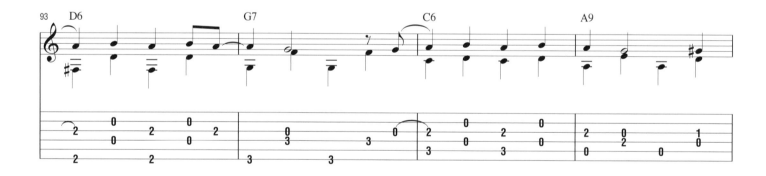

Guitar Notation Legend

Guitar Music can be notated three different ways: on a *musical staff*, in *tablature*, and in *rhythm slashes*.

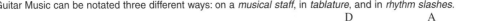

RHYTHM SLASHES are written above the staff. Strum chords in the rhythm indicated. Use the chord diagrams found at the top of the first page of the transcription for the appropriate chord voicings. Round noteheads indicate single notes.

THE MUSICAL STAFF shows pitches and rhythms and is divided by bar lines into measures. Pitches are named after the first seven letters of the alphabet.

TABLATURE graphically represents the guitar fingerboard. Each horizontal line represents a string, and each number represents a fret.

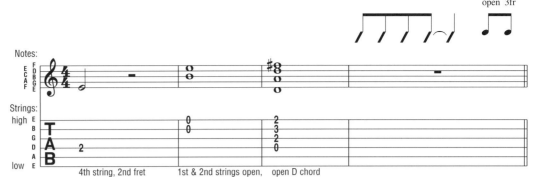

4th string, 2nd fret   1st & 2nd strings open, played together   open D chord

HALF-STEP BEND: Strike the note and bend up 1/2 step.

WHOLE-STEP BEND: Strike the note and bend up one step.

GRACE NOTE BEND: Strike the note and immediately bend up as indicated.

SLIGHT (MICROTONE) BEND: Strike the note and bend up 1/4 step.

BEND AND RELEASE: Strike the note and bend up as indicated, then release back to the original note. Only the first note is struck.

PRE-BEND: Bend the note as indicated, then strike it.

VIBRATO: The string is vibrated by rapidly bending and releasing the note with the fretting hand.

WIDE VIBRATO: The pitch is varied to a greater degree by vibrating with the fretting hand.

HAMMER-ON: Strike the first (lower) note with one finger, then sound the higher note (on the same string) with another finger by fretting it without picking.

PULL-OFF: Place both fingers on the notes to be sounded. Strike the first note and without picking, pull the finger off to sound the second (lower) note.

LEGATO SLIDE: Strike the first note and then slide the same fret-hand finger up or down to the second note. The second note is not struck.

SHIFT SLIDE: Same as legato slide, except the second note is struck.

TRILL: Very rapidly alternate between the notes indicated by continuously hammering on and pulling off.

TAPPING: Hammer ("tap") the fret indicated with the pick-hand index or middle finger and pull off to the note fretted by the fret hand.

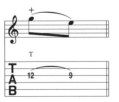

NATURAL HARMONIC: Strike the note while the fret-hand lightly touches the string directly over the fret indicated.

PINCH HARMONIC: The note is fretted normally and a harmonic is produced by adding the edge of the thumb or the tip of the index finger of the pick hand to the normal pick attack.

PICK SCRAPE: The edge of the pick is rubbed down (or up) the string, producing a scratchy sound.

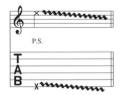

MUFFLED STRINGS: A percussive sound is produced by laying the fret hand across the string(s) without depressing, and striking them with the pick hand.

PALM MUTING: The note is partially muted by the pick hand lightly touching the string(s) just before the bridge.

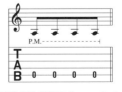

RAKE: Drag the pick across the strings indicated with a single motion.

TREMOLO PICKING: The note is picked as rapidly and continuously as possible.

VIBRATO BAR DIVE AND RETURN: The pitch of the note or chord is dropped a specified number of steps (in rhythm) then returned to the original pitch.

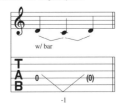

VIBRATO BAR SCOOP: Depress the bar just before striking the note, then quickly release the bar.

VIBRATO BAR DIP: Strike the note and then immediately drop a specified number of steps, then release back to the original pitch.